Contents

Eight in Ten
Adult Learners in Further Education

The Report of the Independent
Committee of Enquiry invited by the
National Institute of Adult Continuing Education
to review the state of adult learning
in colleges of further education in England

©2005 National Institute of Adult Continuing Education
(England and Wales)

21 De Montfort Street
Leicester
LE1 7GE

Company registration no. 2603322
Charity registration no. 1002775

You can find NIACE online at:
www.niace.org.uk

ISBN: 1 86201 278 4

Designed and typeset by Boldface, London
Printed and bound in the UK

Chairman's Foreword

 This Report argues the case for new thinking and new vocabulary to formulate policy and provision for adult learners. Our lives and careers are not linear. Learning for life means dumping old distinctions between initial and continuing education, accredited and informal learning. That so much of the work in the Learning and Skills sector can only be described officially as 'other' tells its own story.

There is a Minister for lifelong learning, but we have no strategy for lifelong learning. The Government's Skills Strategy enjoys broad support. Investment in a well-educated workforce is now accepted as a prerequisite for economic success. But what happened to the argument for a well-educated citizenry?

In these testing times, in which affluence sits side by side with social injustice and as we struggle to achieve equality of outcomes in a diverse but divided society, we need new education strategies to help us all learn to be, as well as learn to know and to do.

I was delighted to Chair this Committee of Enquiry. The members were a formidable bunch. Our meetings were robust, lively and productive. The emergence of a consensus from this group is remarkable and adds huge weight to this report.

Many thanks to them for all their time, knowledge and creativity. And also to NIACE who initiated the Enquiry and supported it throughout. It was a delight to work again with Colin Flint, who deserves considerable credit for the final outcome.

Chris Hughes CBE

Executive Summary

The remit of the Committee was to review the current provision of learning opportunities for adult learners in colleges of further education (FE) in England, and to advise on the projected effects of changed planning and funding strategies. In addition, members were invited to provide advice on:

- the current position of adult learners in FE
- the longer-term implications of current policy and skills strategies
- trends in participation, and identified concerns
- the demand for adult learning in FE
- successful initiatives in widening participation
- recommendations for further action.

The Committee has sought to review current arrangements for adults in colleges, and the challenges posed by the changing demands that adults are likely to make on the sector as a result of demographic and technological change. Members fully support the Skills Strategy and the determined efforts being made by the Government to tackle the longstanding skills deficits from which the country suffers. They recognise the important contribution which the Level 2 entitlement and the Employer Training Pilots are making, and the essential gains being achieved through Skills for Life. However, there has been evidence of an emerging crisis in provision for adults outside of programmes of study contributing to the Skills for Life and Level 2 targets.

For a large proportion of our respondents there are significant reductions in the budgets available for work with adults in 2005-6 while for others there are significant reductions on the budgets anticipated in the three-year planning cycle. The widespread cuts experienced by colleges for their adult learning programmes derive from the low priority afforded to this work. The rise in the 16-18-year-old cohort, which continues until 2009, and the increased numbers staying in education and training, combined with the legislative commitment to meet 16-18s' needs first, have reduced budgets available for adults. This has been exacerbated by the Government's policy commitment to expand school sixth form provision, which attracts a premium to similar work in colleges. Budgets for 'other education' have been further hit by the commitment to prioritise spending on the National Employment Training Pilots, Level 2 and basic skills.

The Enquiry recognises that government policy seeks to secure increased contributions from adults who can afford to pay, studying outside of priority areas, and that it seeks increased investment in education and training from employers. In the Committee's view, neither aspiration is currently backed by practical measures to secure the desired outcomes.

Adults with learning difficulties and disabilities are at particular risk – first of being offered a diet of Skills for Life provision and little else; second, from the increasing focus in Skills for Life only on provision which is likely to lead to qualifications that contribute to the targets.

There is too much variability in advice, and inconsistent levels of understanding by staff in local Learning and Skills Councils (LSCs) overseeing planning decisions about adult learning. We have been surprised at how little Government and LSC thinking, or Sector Skills Council planning, have so far addressed the impact demographic change must have on the labour market and the post-school education and training system over the next decade.

We have been struck, too, by the absence of an explicit focus on adults in the internal planning arrangements in the majority of colleges, and recommend that the development of a clear focus on adults will help colleges plan effectively for their needs over the next decade.

There is widespread recognition that the funding situation will worsen in 2006-7 and 2007-8, while the demographic bulge continues, and the full impact of the policy changes deriving from the Skills Strategy and the 14-19 policies take effect. There is, it is clear, an urgent need to rebalance budgets to avoid erosion of the complex First Steps learning opportunities that many adults use as a springboard to more sustained study, and as a source of continuing education. There is an equally urgent need to find additional funding for 2006-7 if the Skills Strategy is not to be put at risk through the unplanned consequences of current priorities.

Our evidence suggests that measures which work to create a more adult-friendly environment for colleges also work well for young people not currently in education, employment or training who are seeking to re-engage with learning.

As is made clear in the body of the Report, the Committee has discussed the central mission of further education and its implication for adults. It is seen as the provision of vocational education to adults and to young people beyond the age of compulsory schooling; and to provide related learning opportunities accessible to all who can benefit. The discussions of the Committee led to the conclusion that there should be clearer focus for adult learning in colleges. The concept of three major themes forms part of the Recommendations, and is developed in the body of the Report.

Our main Conclusions and Recommendations follow, but action is also necessary in the following areas:

- the need for more strategic collaboration between colleges, businesses, community organisations, local authorities and LSCs
- the need for college staff to reclaim a sense of agency and authority in curriculum and qualification design, delivery and assessment
- performance indicators which measure public value in more effective ways than is currently the case
- a greater awareness of multiculturalism and cultural diversity
- overcoming unhelpful divisions, whether between vocational and academic programmes and institutions or between learners of

different ages, which impair the motivation of learners and impede the meeting of workforce and employer needs

- the limited effectiveness of integration between Adult Learning Grants and other benefits which restricts levels of take-up
- the levels of bureaucracy associated with brokerage arrangements for work-related training which may hinder rather than facilitate participation
- the avoidance of damage to the infrastructure of provision for adult learning
- over-precipitate introduction of change without time for sufficient social and cultural repositioning and adjustment.

The Report seeks to make recommendations which, if incorporated into subsequent policy, will secure and improve opportunities for adult learners in a broad range of provision. It presents the findings of the research which supported and informed the deliberations of the Committee along with the evidence heard from the witnesses and drawn from the case studies, and comments both on the present circumstances in which the colleges perform their functions in adult learning and on possible futures. In short, the Report details what we found, and what we believe needs to be done.

It presents its **vision of the key themes of adult learning** for the next ten or more years; an **overview of the college sector** and of the adults now using it; the **policy challenge** facing the country and the colleges; and the essential reforms which will be necessary to support the new vision, in the areas of **qualifications and assessment**, and of the **funding of adult learning**. It concludes with a plea for a return to a renewed conceptualisation of **lifelong learning**, which can and should underpin all of our strategies and policies for adults.

The Committee commends its report to the Department for Education and Skills, to the LSC, to the colleges and to all with an interest in the future of adult learning.

Conclusions and Recommendations

The new framework
Adult learning in colleges should focus on three key areas, and should be made the basis of the planning and funding of adult provision

- Access to employability
- Workforce development
- Creating and sustaining cultural value.

There should be a new statutory basis for the funding of adult learning which is not contingent upon other needs and which has its own priority.

Adult learning is central to the work of many Government departments. This needs to be recognised in an over-arching coordinated direction of policy.

There should be a lifelong learning strategy, to complement that for skills.

The adult learners and their needs
The Level 2 entitlement should be reframed to include all relevant learning up to and including the Level 2 qualification. We believe there is a strong case for a Level 3 entitlement for adults without such a qualification.

The proposed system of credit-based qualifications should be introduced as a matter of greater urgency than is currently envisaged.

There is need for coherent policy and guidance on course fees in further education.

Consideration should be given to the introduction of career development loans for full-time students in further education.

The colleges

The strategic role of colleges should be recognised and confirmed in planning and funding policy in post-16 education. The role and purposes of local LSC offices should be reviewed and redefined.

There should be a discretionary element in the core funding of colleges, so that they can respond to locally-determined need. Post hoc accountability mechanisms should be developed for this funding strand.

Leadership and public image of the colleges need urgent attention and improvement if they are to fulfil their potential and justify a lead role in economic and social development. Both image and reputation would be enhanced if they exercised greater leadership in arguing the case for older learners, displaying the same authority and confidence as when pursuing claims for better funding.

1
A new vision

1. Eight in ten students in further education colleges are adults over the age of 19. Adults account for 50 per cent of the taught learning hours in colleges, and colleges provide 85 per cent of the provision funded by the Learning and Skills Council. Yet adults, other than those without vocational qualifications or requiring basic skills training, seem largely invisible in the policy-making that shapes post-school education in England, whether in the legislative arrangements that shape the sector, or in the concerns expressed by politicians or policy-makers, by institutional heads, or by the press. Current strategies seem to ignore the fact that two in three of the new and replacement job vacancies over the next decade will be filled by adults, since the cohort of young people entering the labour market will not be large enough.

2. Despite a rhetorical commitment to the notion of lifelong learning and the widely-shared understanding that it is a significant contributor to the creation of a fairer, more cohesive and more inclusive society, the dominant drivers of Government policy are clearly designed to improve the preparation of first-time entrants to the labour market and to help less well-qualified adults to qualifications which may enhance their employability. In all the discussion it is clear that the greatest influences on public policy are the drives to:
   - increase the proportion of teenagers who extend their initial education or training beyond the minimum school-leaving age
   - reduce the number of people dependent on welfare benefits
   - increase the proportion of the population in paid employment

● improve skill levels among the working population.

3. While giving whole-hearted support to these necessary and ambitious objectives, concerns were felt about the possible consequences to much other important work with adult learners. In this context NIACE established an Independent Enquiry, chaired by Chris Hughes, the former Chief Executive of the Learning and Skills Development Agency, to consider how best the interests of adult learners might be met in further education colleges. The Committee, whose membership is listed at the end of this Report, met seven times, took evidence from 11 witnesses, received 140 written submissions in response to a questionnaire sent to all FE colleges, undertook a literature survey and data search, and made an interim submission to Sir Andrew Foster's enquiry into the future of further education, undertaken for the LSC and the Department for Education and Skills.

4. While the Committee was meeting, widespread concerns were expressed about the prospects for the funding of adult learning in 2005-6, and in particular for the two subsequent years. A number of the submissions received focused on the pressures on college provision for adults deriving from a short-term bulge in the numbers of young people in further education – a demographic blip that will work through FE by 2009 – and from improvements in the participation rates among young people; coupled with the impact of the changing priorities of Government funding following on from the Skills Strategy, and the introduction of Employer Training Pilots.

5. The Committee was keen to identify key features of the role of colleges in meeting adult learners' needs over the next 15 years, and to suggest what might be done about barriers in current arrangements that inhibit this role.

6. In its interim report, the Committee identified the key mission of further education colleges as: the provision of vocational education to adults and to young people beyond the age of compulsory schooling. It stands by that broad definition of mission now, though recognising that colleges contribute significantly to the achievement

of other educational objectives, as in their work in general education and in higher education. However, the Committee identified three key themes in the work that colleges undertake with adults that will need to be central to their continuing function. These are:

● **Access to employability**, including 'welfare to work' programmes; the provision of support for literacy, language and numeracy; provision recently characterised as 'First Steps', offering progression routes to Level 2 qualifications; and initiatives to secure effective support to enable marginalised groups to undertake learning which successfully supports access to labour markets.

● **Workforce development**, supporting employers and employees in developing skills, knowledge and understanding to enhance business success, individual opportunity in existing jobs and career development through learning programmes offered in and outside the workplace; supporting trade union learning initiatives; and encouraging new and emerging enterprises through initiatives to foster innovation and entrepreneurship.

● **Creating and sustaining cultural value**, providing learning opportunities that foster a critical and informed engagement with social, political and moral issues, and thus support the development of a tolerant, participative democracy for all citizens and communities; that encourage appreciation and participation in the arts, sport and cultural activities; and that secure the role learning can play in the achievement of public and collective good.

7. The Committee recognises that other agencies, private voluntary and public, will have roles to play in the achievement of each of these goals, alone or in partnership with colleges. Individual institutions will shape the balance of their offer in the light of other agencies' activities. But the Committee is convinced that all are important to the range and reach of the college mission.

8. In addition to the three themes identified above, the Committee concluded that a key function of colleges is and will continue to be to support the learning dimensions of cross-Government initiatives affecting adults. The research findings of the Research Centre on the Wider Benefits of Learning highlight the impact learning can have on

the health and well-being of adults, and the national strategy for mental health recognises the importance of learning in promoting positive mental health, and in re-engaging people recovering from periods of mental illness. Learning has a central role in the Home Office's citizenship programmes, and in the work of its Active Communities Unit. It is central to the active labour market strategies of the Department of Work and Pensions, and to the financial education strategies that underpin the Department's approach to modernising pensions arrangements. The Department of Culture, Media and Sport recognises the importance of lifelong learning in the work of cultural institutions and of broadcasting. The Office of the Deputy Prime Minister is concerned with neighbourhood renewal, and with local government's responsibilities to foster the welfare of communities. The Department of Trade and Industry is concerned with business success and with innovation. Colleges' work with adults enriches each of these dimensions of government policy, in addition to the explicit focus of its work in supporting vocational education for adults and young people. We have been promised 'joined-up government'. There is a clear need for it in this arena.

9. The Committee noted the movement across government to shorten the chain between policy formation and front-line service delivery. At the same time, developments in post-school education and training have tended strongly to centralise planning and policy-making. It believes that effective provision for the current and future needs of adult learners will require a re-assertion of the strategic role of colleges, and a proportionate restoration of freedom to respond to demand in local communities and businesses. The Committee recognises the importance of centrally-determined goals in shaping the expenditure of public money, but also that centrally-shaped public policy is too often a blunt instrument, for example in relation to higher education developments in further education, in provision for apprentices, in fees strategy, and in the current response to pressures on adult budgets. The Committee believes that a proper balance needs to be struck. It recommends that at least 20 per cent of colleges' budgets should be at college discretion, with accountability for use after the event. The implication of this is that

the role of local LSCs will need to be significantly circumscribed. It cannot be sensible for key decisions about the balance of learning needs in local communities to be taken by generalist administrators, often at quite a junior level, rather than on the judgment of educational professionals with a lifetime's experience.

10. The Committee has noted that recent announcements (September 2005) concerning a major restructuring of the LSC may foreshadow significant changes in its local and regional organisation, and that there may be important implications for providers. The LSC's *Agenda for Change*, recently detailed, will also clearly affect the learning environment. The proposed employer-accredited Quality mark will certainly be a powerful incentive to colleges to strengthen and promote their work-related activities. The proposal to channel £40 million, saved through cuts in administration and bureaucracy, into the provision of learning is unreservedly welcomed.

2
Overview

The college sector

11. England's 397 colleges comprise the largest part of the learning and skills sector, both in terms of their budgets (in total nearly £4.8 billion out of the total Learning and Skills Council spend of £8.8 billion in 2003-4) and in terms of student numbers (four million students).

12. Colleges are extraordinarily diverse institutions – ranging from monotechnics to complex federal bodies. Some, serving scattered rural communities, are almost the only source of publicly-funded post-school provision. Some operate budgets in excess of £40m. Others operate in a complex market among a multiplicity of other providers. They work in prisons, hospices, community centres and workplaces as well as in dedicated educational buildings.

13. Characteristically, the general FE colleges (GFEs), of which there are 257, recruit a wider social and economic mix of students than other providers: colleges have taken to heart the challenges posed in Baroness Kennedy's report for the Further Education Funding Council (*Learning Works*, 1997). They have made the most significant contribution to the widening of opportunity in recent years, and continue to do so. The Committee believes this to be essential work.

14. Colleges operate in a crowded environment. Their principal source of finance is the LSC, which was established following the Learning and

Skills Act in 2000, with a national office and 47 local Councils. Subsequent reorganisation has strengthened the LSC's regional structure. The Council has a duty to plan and fund sufficient education and training for young people aged 16-19, and reasonable provision for adults. The Act defines *'reasonable'* in this context as *'what the Council decides is reasonable in the light of the resources available to it.'* There is likely to be a serious shortage of resource in the foreseeable future.

15. Other agencies have a significant impact on colleges. Regional Development Agencies (RDAs) have increasingly sought to address their economic development responsibilities through a concern with skills policies. Twenty-five Sector Skills Councils (SSCs), covering more than 80 per cent of the workforce and led by employers' representatives, have been given a leading responsibility for shaping skills development in their industry sectors. The Higher Education Funding Council for England funds higher education provision in further education colleges, and around 11 per cent of all English higher education is delivered in them. The European Union's European Social Fund co-finances provision targeting people disadvantaged in the labour market, and in comparatively disadvantaged regions (though this will diminish markedly from 2007 when the current funding round ends). Local education authorities retain a significant role – often as the largest employer, and potential purchaser of college services, but also as a provider (or commissioner) of further education through adult and community learning and mainstream FE budgets. Private sector training providers and voluntary and community sector providers also draw on LSC funding – and there is a large, wholly commercial, private sector operating in some curriculum areas, where markets can sustain them.

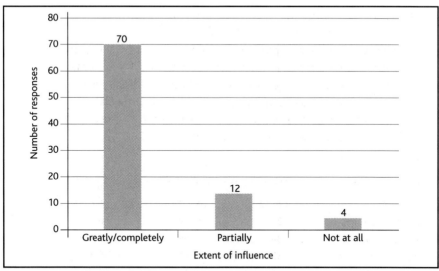

Figure 1: Perceived influence of current DfES/LSC priorities on college planning.
Source: NIACE Consultation Questionnaire

CASE STUDY B

Example of a college withdrawing from part-time adult work to focus upon LSC priorities. In their IT Skills Centre they have never been able to charge full fees because of the fee policies of learndirect. As the provision is 'other', it will be cut.

GENERAL FE COLLEGE IN THE NW AND CASE STUDY C

GSCE pass rates more than 10 per cent under the national average, and 39 per cent of adults don't have a qualification. Because of this they have an increasing number of progressing 19-year-olds – these are students who simply take longer to achieve. The college thinks that these will fall foul of the age split – as they will need to finish their courses as adults. To fund these students, as they must do because they have a commitment to them, the college will have to cut Level 2, Skills for Life, employer-related provision, as well as 'FE Other' programmes for adults.

Where are the adults?

16. Colleges are the major providers of publicly-funded adult opportunities in England. As Table 1 shows, there are five times as many
adults as under-19s in general further education colleges, and the
ratio is almost the same in the sector as a whole. Even Sixth Form
Colleges have more than 40 per cent of participants who are over 19,
though these are mainly full-time students in their 20th year.

Table 1: Enrolments/attendance in FE by age, 2003–4. Student numbers in thousands

	Under 19	Over 19	All
General FE Colleges	524	2,499	3,023
Sixth Form Colleges	134	95	229
External Institutions	38	711	749
Other Colleges	5	108	113
FE Sector Total	701	3,413	4,114

Source: DfES analysis, Individual Learner Record (ILR) data 2003–4

Among these learners, a great majority of adults study part-time, as
Table 2 shows.

Table 2: Mode of study for 19+ learners, thousands enrolled, 2003–4

	Full-time	Part-time	Total
General FE Colleges	347	2,152	2,499
Sixth Form Colleges	8	87	95

Source: DfES analysis, ILR data, 2003–4

17. By contrast, 401,000 of the 524,000 under-19 learners in general FE
colleges study full-time, and their needs and success rates are,
inevitably and properly, a prime focus of Government and LSC
attention. Unfortunately, the effect of this is to risk making much of
the work of colleges in meeting the needs of adults at best marginal,
at worst invisible to their overall planning and policy directions.

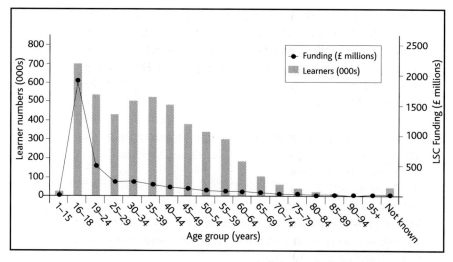

Figure 2: LSC Funding and student numbers for learning in FE, ACL and UfI, 2003-4

18. As well as being very substantially part-time, much of adults' study is concentrated at the lowest level of qualification aim, a clear indication of the backlog of under-achievement among a large proportion of the adult population. Many of these learners, as well as high proportions of non-participants, are not ready for Level 2. Of the 3,413,000 over-19s in further education, almost one and a quarter million are over 50 – highlighting the role FE plays in later career transitions, as well as the success of the BiteSize initiative in stimulating older people's participation.

Table 3: Proportion (%) of overall student enrolment by age group and qualification aim

Qualification aim	19 and under	19+
Entry and Level 1	3	36
Level 2	4	21
Level 3	9	11
Levels 4/5/HE	0	2
Level not specified	0	13
Total	17	83

Source: ILR/SFR05 (14 December 2004) Note: excludes external institutions

19. Women constitute a significant majority of further education learners (2,500,000 of the 4,100,000 overall); and 14 per cent of the further education adult population is non-white, which is double the proportion in the general national adult population. Fifty-seven per cent of learners have been eligible for the Learning and Skills Council's uplift ratio.

20. Colleges have a significant and proud record in meeting the learning aspirations of groups and communities otherwise under-represented in the post-compulsory education and training system. This is a vital social role as well as an educational one and it is essential that, in terms of national aspirations for social inclusion and multicultural harmonies, this work should continue to be recognised. A recent authoritative publication emphasises afresh the enduring role that social class plays in British society:

    "those from routine or lower supervisory backgrounds are...more likely not to be in employment, education or training (the so-called NEET category.) This group faces poorer prospects for the rest of their lives, which cannot be reconciled with a commitment to equality of opportunity. It should be of particular concern that the number of people who are NEET has remained relatively unchanged since 1997."

    Social Justice: Building a Fairer Britain. Ed. Pearce and Paxton, IPPR, 2005

21. Adult student satisfaction indices are markedly better than those for young people, and their achievement rates (48 per cent against 40 per cent at Level 2) are also significantly better. High levels of satisfaction with the learning experience in further education are recorded in the most recent LSC survey. The overwhelming volume of expansion in the further education sector from 2000-1 was concentrated in part-time adult learning, and on short courses in particular.

What do adults study?

22. There are marked differences between adults and under-19s in the pattern of courses undertaken (see Table 4), with a strong concentration of adult participation in information and communications technology, foundation programmes, health, social care and public services, and business administration, management and professional services.

Table 4: Area of learning – proportion of learning aims (%)

	16-19		20 and over	
	2002-2003	2003-2004	2002-2003	2003-2004
Science and mathematics	12	11	4	3
Land-based provision	1	1	1	2
Construction	2	2	3	3
Engineering, technology and manufacturing	3	3	3	3
Business administration, management and professional	6	5	11	9
Information and communications technology	12	11	24	19
Retailing, customer service and transportation	1	0	2	1
Hospitality, sports, leisure and travel	6	6	6	7
Hairdressing and beauty therapy	2	2	3	2
Health, social care and public services	6	6	12	14
Visual and performing arts and media	7	8	6	7
Humanities	10	10	3	3
English, languages and communication	12	12	5	5
Foundation programmes	10	12	13	18
Not known	11	12	4	5

Source: ILR

Worthy of note is the small volume of adult participation in science and mathematics (where the contrast with younger learners is striking), and in areas where colleges have traditionally played a central vocational role – in construction, engineering, technology and manufacturing, and retailing, customer service, and transportation.

23. In part, the reason for this balance of recruitment (which contrasts strikingly with the overall representation of different sectors in the economy) may lie in the funding mechanism in place in the 1990s which discouraged colleges from persevering with curriculum areas with cyclically-depressed curriculum demand. In part it may reflect the relative inflexibility of college funding in enabling institutions to respond to the just-in-time and customised learning opportunities demanded by many private sector providers. In part, too, the pattern reflects colleges' relative success in developing vocational routes from an expanding public sector economy, and their responsiveness to the growing importance of financial and business services, new technologies and management as employment routes.

24. It can be surmised that the figures also highlight the difficulty many adult workers experience in persuading employers to fund their skills development, particularly in small and medium-sized enterprises in the private sector. It should be noted that a large volume of vocational activity is aimed at adults, with 1,772,569 adult learners in colleges in 2002-3 (ILR Data). Many of these (711,656) were studying at Entry Level or Level 1 – more than at any other level (see Figure 3).

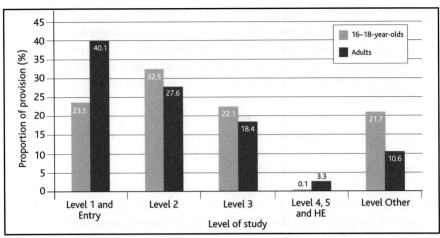

Figure 3: Vocational provision for 16-18-year-olds and adults, by level of study.
Source: ILR, 2003-4

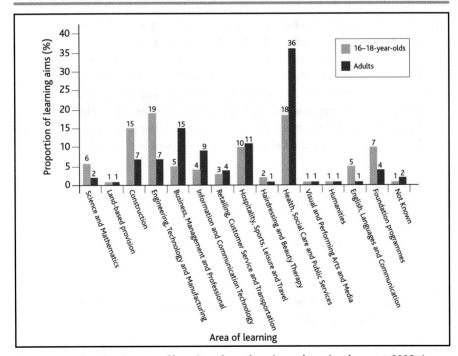

Figure 4: Learning aims in areas of learning where there is employer involvement, 2003-4. There were 71,064 learning aims for 16-19-year-olds and 536,339 for adults (*Source*: ILR).

25. By a considerable margin, the largest proportion of adult vocational learners supported by their employers are studying in the health, social care and public services area of learning. This is the largest single group of employer-supported learners, either adult or 16-19, in FE. Other areas where there is a significant adult presence are business administration, management and professional, hospitality, and ICT. These four areas of learning (but also retailing, customer services and transportation) are proportionately more significant to adult learners than they are to 16-19-year-olds. In all other areas, 16-19-year-olds are in the majority.

26. The evidence lends some support to the view expressed by a manager in Case Study A, that the critical factor for employer engagement is the presence of a large, public sector employer who is willing to support learning.

27. Given this pattern of provision, it is perhaps unsurprising that so many of the 100-plus senior managers in further education surveyed by NIACE for this Report put emphasis on the support and development of individuals as the principal function of further education as they saw it. A much smaller number cited community support as a key role, and less than one in ten saw support for the economy as a primary role – though the role in supporting individuals obviously does not preclude supporting the economy as well.

As one respondent to our survey said:

"I have always seen FE as the land of second chance. We take failures, the redundant, the poorly-educated and change their lives (for a fraction of the cost of schools or universities)."

Or, as another one put it:

"It [FE] provides a wide range of learning opportunities, particularly for those who did not benefit too well from school."

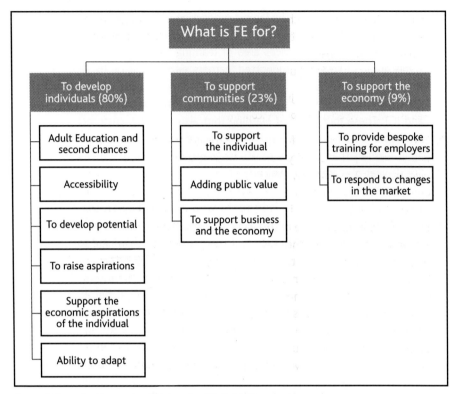

Figure 5. A service focused on the needs of individuals
College managers' responses to the question "What is FE for?"
NB: The responses to this question are not mutually exclusive, and so will total more
than 100 per cent.

28. Almost a quarter of respondents suggested that their role was to support communities. This role embraced a complex range of aims: to meet the needs of the individual, to support business, and to contribute to the maintenance and development of civic culture and cohesion. This last point is critical. Over and above the direct contribution that education makes to society through, for example, the gaining of qualifications and the impact upon the employability that this has for individuals, there are other positive outcomes of education – often referred to as the wider benefits of learning, and 'Public Value'. An FE college is an important civic institution, and

evidence from our research suggests that successful colleges have relevance and influence in the lives of people within their local areas to a remarkable degree.

As a third correspondent put it:

"[FE's] purpose includes social justice, equity, and learning for its own sake, as well as a support mechanism for the economy."

29. The concern for learning for its own sake generated considerable debate during the Enquiry. As several witnesses pointed out in evidence to the Enquiry, much government policy on further education is utilitarian in tone, and narrowly focused on hitting targets. As a result, it often ignores the wider work carried out by the FE sector. Indeed, the value of this work may also tend to receive less attention from colleges themselves, as they strive to pursue DfES priorities. In consequence there are examples of unacceptably high levels of inadequacy in some of this type of provision, with up to a third of adult and community learning classes judged less than adequate. There is a serious message here not only for those colleges whose provision is weak but also for the whole sector: if the quality of this area of provision is unsatisfactory, the case for it to be seen as an important part of the work of colleges is seriously compromised.

Students with learning difficulties and disabilities

30. There is a particular issue in relation to the mission of FE in respect of adult learners with learning difficulties. Although there is a statutory protection of the needs of such students, enshrined in the legislation that set up both the LSC and its predecessor, the Further Education Funding Council, the provision is at risk in a number of colleges because, at a time of reduced funding for work with adults, such provision costs more than standard work. The NIACE survey found four colleges intending to cut their provision completely and a further 13 cutting the level of support to this group of students – this out of the first 100 colleges responding.

CASE STUDY B

They are thinking about threatening to cut SLDD. This will demonstrate gravity of situation to LSC. This college will not continue to subsidise provision out of a sense of public duty!

CASE STUDY C

College had paid travel for disabled students, and this will end.

CASE STUDY D

Most SLDD at pre-entry level. Some had been mapped to basic skills curriculum, but provision for independent living skills is high-cost, and will be hard to protect. Cutting this provision will have a knock on other public services, like social services, mental health services, and so on.

Some courses in British Sign Language and in Lip-reading – vital to support SLDD students – are being cut or priced out of the reach of most learners. There is likely to be a serious shortage of support workers. (NIACE Questionnaire)

31. The contrast between colleges' perceptions of their existing strengths, on the one hand, and the balance of current Government and funding council priorities, on the other, is striking, as may be seen by contrasting Figures 5 and 6.

This envisages a sector strongly influenced by funding priorities in order to maintain stable funding. Respondents described their dilemmas in meeting these priorities:

"Concentrating the mind on achieving a balance between funding priorities and non-accredited provision. What to keep? If putting on new provision does it fit Government/LSC agenda? If no, should I go ahead?"

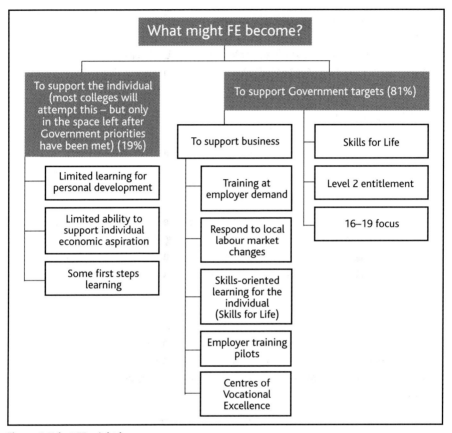

Figure 6: What FE might become

"Makes us focus on 14-19 and NLSC priority areas, not necessarily on meeting local needs."

"We are becoming more of a full 16-19 college – currently 75% [of our students] moving to 90%."

"Current funding and planning priorities have influenced the focus of curriculum development and the utilisation of already scarce resources. There has been a shift in focus from needs-led learner-centred provision to economically viable accredited provision. Following LSC recommendations and guidelines the college will give increased priority to learners 16-19; [and] reduce provision which is designated 'other'..."

The colleges' workforce

32. Meeting the Government's priorities to the degree that is necessary, while continuing to address individual and community needs, will present a challenge to college staff, who are themselves as a workforce subject to the same demographic changes that affect the wider economy.

Table 5. The FE workforce (number of teachers)

Full-time	49,000
Part-time	85,000
Total	133,000

Of the entire FE workforce, 52 per cent are aged 45+, 34 per cent aged 50+, 15 per cent aged 55+ and 4 per cent aged 60+. Just one in two is in a permanent contract.

33. Further education colleges, like the economy more widely, face the challenge of reorganisation and culture change with an ageing workforce, many of whom combine high levels of dedication to students with demoralisation about the value afforded to their work by a wider community. While the challenge is also an opportunity, it is highly likely that significant financial strain is going to be put on colleges as the balance of their work changes, and it may be necessary for hypothecated funding to be made available to support these processes.

34. In whatever changes are going to be required of further education in the next phases of the development of the colleges, their work will continue to be with adults as well as with young people. A thorough understanding of these considerations will continue to be a pre-requisite of successful work with adult learners.

Are adult learners different?

35. **A significant proportion of adult participation is in studies for personal fulfilment and community development, and the need for this will grow.** There is powerful evidence of the positive health effects (important for an ageing population) and the rise of civic engagement that result from participation in adult learning of all sorts. Ministers are keen to preserve this dimension of further education – as Gordon Brown puts it, we must meet the needs not only of people as they are, but also of whom they might become. There is both a social justice and an economic rationale for investing in these wider benefits of learning, not least in savings on the health budget and in crime reduction. Many adults will contribute a significant proportion of costs of such provision – but budget pressures currently put much of the provision at risk.

36. **Many adults are alienated from structured education and training** Between a quarter and a third of adults say they have done no formal learning since school, and 85 per cent of them think it unlikely that they will participate in the future – yet there is nothing inevitable about this, and their engagement is important both on economic grounds and for social inclusion. Good practice in widening participation abounds, with colleges more successful than other educational institutions in providing successfully for working-class students in particular. Most current adult students study at or below Level 2, and choose colleges to get help to lead a more confident life, to get or keep a job, or to get a better job. But like responsiveness to the needs of employers, successful engagement of the hardest-to-reach groups is difficult to secure through current public support arrangements. Indeed, current policy changes risk losing much that is good and effective in widening participation, and in securing achievement and progression routes that work for the least qualified adults. This was a major concern both for Committee members and for respondents to the NIACE survey.

37. **Adult learners are untidy, as are employers' needs.** Adults fit learning alongside the other demands in their lives. As a result, they

often study in short bursts, pursue development through a pattern of studies hard to equate with vertical progression routes, drop out for a while (creating havoc with progression and retention) and re-engage, often using different institutions. Some adults choose to learn intensively for short periods. Employers, too, often seek short episodes of learning for their staff, which do not sit easily with conventional educational structures. Good providers of effective teaching and learning recognise this.

38. **Adults are different – they bring a greater volume and range of experience to their studies than young people can.** This gives them potentially greater resources to draw on, and a set of external criteria against which to measure the value of the educational experience. Many also bring negative experiences of previous education. Effective teaching and learning strategies build on the positive experiences.

39. **Adults' motivation in learning is often more complex and their objectives more individual than those of young people.** Most adults take part in education and training voluntarily. However, when adults are supported in their studies by employers, colleges are faced with two customers, whose needs and demands may not be the same. As a priority, the DfES work on personalisation in schools must be paralleled in work with adults in colleges. This work should build on FE work on inclusive learning, and focus on linking learning to individual starting points, aspirations and learning capacity.

Promoting the case

40. Colleges that work successfully with adults know and practise all of this, but the challenge to them is to make the case for the work that they do with adult learners much more strongly. The colleges of further education give a service to something of the order of 3.5 million adult learners a year, and most of that number rate the provision they receive very positively. But the voice of the college sector, either individually or collectively, is rarely heard in forceful argument about the vital nature of this work, about the indivisibility

of economic prosperity, social cohesion and an educated society. There are complaints about cuts in funding but it is the intellectual and the educational argument that needs to be won, and it is one that should not be limited to skills development. Skills for social justice should be seen as being as important as those for economic strength

41. The colleges will need to demonstrate their belief in the value of the work that they do with adult learners much more effectively than in the recent past. Work with adults is **not** marginal.

CASE STUDY B

The fundamental nature of the college is being changed from a GFE college serving the needs of the local area (through part-time learning opportunities, community outreach activities) to a daytime 16-19 college, as a result of priorities. It is no longer able to do what its governing body wants it to do.

CASE STUDY C

The college came out of recovery in 2004 with a plan for growth (discussed with LSC), now there is no funding available for growth. Principal appointed for growth, and governors now 'astonished' that goalposts have changed in-year. They have over-achieved on enrolments, but are not funded to run courses. The character of colleges is being changed by Government priorities, not governors. The ability of colleges to act strategically is being undermined.

3

The policy challenge

Key themes and trends

42. *International competition*

    The context in which colleges work is changing rapidly. Successive waves of newly industrialising countries have put pressure on the economies of Western Europe and the United States to accelerate technological innovation and to intensify productivity to maintain competitiveness in a growing global economy. The different elements of product development and design, production, distribution and marketing are increasingly often distributed internationally. The speed of development of the Chinese and Indian economies has recently intensified this process.

43. *Productivity*

    Despite a decade of relative economic success, and of consistently high levels of employment, productivity levels in the UK remain stubbornly below those of Germany, France and the USA. Successive governments since the early 1980s have sought to address what the CBI described as 'the long tail of under-achievement' through a variety of supply-side reforms, the establishment of national targets for qualifications achievement, and renewed focus on learning at work. At the same time there has been substantial new investment in higher education and the establishment and subsequent overhaul of a national curriculum in schools. Few believe that this has yet secured an end to the academic-vocational divide that has bedevilled British education for more than a century. The latest initiative to address this concern produced Sir Mike Tomlinson's proposals on 14-19 reform, and the Government's agreement to pursue vocational diplomas for that age group. Many engaged in education think that the latest proposals do not go far enough.

44. *Skills*

The adoption of the Skills for Life Strategy in 2001, the Skills Strategy in 2003, and its update in 2005 focused public policy priorities for post-compulsory further education on the needs of those with fewest skills. The Government recognised market failure at Level 2 – the level of skills a successful 16-year-old might achieve – and accepted the need to invest public funding to address this by offering learners an entitlement to free education to gain a first full Level 2. In addition, the Government recognised that literacy, language and numeracy work below Level 2 should be fully funded by the state. Some of the pressures colleges currently face derive from the failure, as yet, to secure a new balance of funding in which individuals, employers and the state all invest more in education. The case for this investment remains to be made persuasively to many employers and to individuals who learned early that 'education is for other people'. Issues around funding and fees are explored at greater length later in the report.

45. *Social mobility*

The intensification of focus on skills policy has, to an extent at least, taken attention away from the Government's earlier focus on seeking to reinforce social cohesion through its lifelong learning policies. Recent evidence makes clear that despite increased investment in education and training, there has been a reduction in social mobility. As Ruth Kelly observed in a recent Fabian Society lecture, 'If you were born in the 1970s, then what your parents did had more of a bearing on your life chances than if you were born in the 1950s'. It is a central aspiration of Government policy now to reverse that trend.

46. *Geographic mobility*

If there is little social mobility, there is an increase in geographic mobility, both within the country – where the most qualified gravitate to the high-value added employment opportunities of London and the South East – and internationally. Migration – for asylum, and in pursuit of economic betterment – leads to significant flows of people to and (for economic reasons) from the UK. This poses further challenges to our programmes of English for Speakers of Other Languages, and to our mechanisms for recognising qualifications and experience gained overseas. Some current ESOL provision is at risk of the withdrawal of supporting funding because it is classified as 'other'.

47. *Demographic trends*

The demographic profile of England is changing. Figures from the Office of National Statistics project an increase in the UK population to over 65 million by 2050 before gradually falling. In England, the population is expected to continue increasing for the next 40 years, but at a reduced rate of growth. However, within this overall rise, the proportion of older people in the UK is expected to rise sharply over the coming half century, as shown in Figure 7.

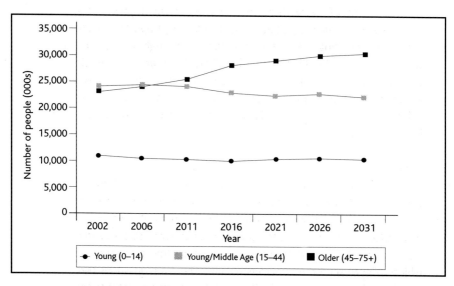

Figure 7: Projected UK population by age, 2002–2031.
Source: Adult Learning at a Glance: UK context, facts and figures 2004 (NIACE, Leicester: 2004)

48. The UK population has an ageing demographic profile. There is currently a bulge of 16-19-year-olds as stated earlier, but this will start to reduce by 2009 (source: ONS). Alongside this there is an increase in the number of older people that will continue over the next few decades – for example the number of 60- to 74-year-olds is predicted to increase by 49.3 per cent by 2031 (*Source: Adult Learning at a Glance: UK context, facts and figures 2004*, NIACE, Leicester: 2004). By 2007, the population of pensionable age is projected to exceed the number of children under 16. Older people will form an increasingly significant element of the population (and the workforce) in coming years.

49. Addressing the skills needs of those over 19 who may *already* be in the workplace will become increasingly important – after all, someone who is an adult now, perhaps 25, will only be 51 in 2031 when there will be a high proportion of 60-to 74-year-olds. If such a person has skills needs he or she would benefit from adult learning in FE *now*, and throughout the projected demographic shifts, up to a possible retirement at the age of 65 in 2045. Between 2002 and 2012 two out of every three new and replacement jobs in the workplace will be filled by adults. It will be critically important not to rely upon redressing the UK's skills imbalance through a concentration solely upon the 16-19-year-old cohort. If we are to maintain international competitiveness, then upgrading the skills of those *already* in the work place must be a clear and immediate priority, as will the engagement and upskilling of adults currently outside the labour market.

50. **Public service reform**
    These changes have informed the decision of the Government from the end of the 1990s to increase public sector investment, and to accompany that with public service reform. A variety of initiatives to focus attention on improving the quality of services, and to ensure that investment is focused on frontline services, affect the environment in which colleges and other providers operate. There are questions here too about the strategic role of colleges – who or what is best fitted to lead and develop frontline educational services at a local level?

51. ***Rethinking the college contribution***

    Many adults use colleges: not all of them do so for directly economic purposes. Courses undertaken for leisure or social reasons may lead to a vocational interest, and the benefits of involvement in educational activity are well known. FE colleges make a considerable contribution to the long and honourable traditions of adult education in this country, and have done so for many years. It is part of the civic role of colleges. Facilities, spread of curriculum, deployment of staff and flexibility of planning have made them the natural home for a very wide range of academic, vocational and leisure classes. It would be an immeasurable loss if colleges were no longer able to make such provision – but the quality of such work, in a period of rising course fees and almost certainly of increased competition, will be paramount.

52. ***Difficulty of conceptualising the education and training of adults***

    The richness and diversity of adult learning has resisted easy categorisation for generations, yet it is only since the Further and Higher Education Act that central government has sought to use legislation and regulation to determine the range of courses offered. The earlier Acts of Parliament that developed the further education sector (in 1919 and 1944) made no distinction between classes run for explicitly vocational purposes and those for a broader range of purposes, ranging from arts and crafts to liberal and academic study.

53. What teachers of adults recognise more readily than governments is that the title of a course does not, of itself, explain the motivations of the students following it. While some might enrol on a course for work-related reasons, others will do so for alternative reasons. They may be equally valid, equally beneficial. Reference is made elsewhere to the research on the wider benefits of learning.

54. While the Learning and Skills Act 2000 did away with the distinction between 'Schedule 2' and 'non-Schedule 2' courses, the largely discredited divide has crept back in the form of a distinction between courses within the National Qualifications Framework and what is

described as 'other further education' (a category which in some colleges still constitutes the majority of provision). It is arguably the case that the present situation under the NQF is now worse than under Schedule 2, as it puts much more work with adults under threat. The key issue of the replacement of the NQF by the proposed credit-based Framework for Achievement is dealt with later in this Report.

55. What is clear is that any typology that introduces ever-finer distinctions among certain sorts of learning but lumps the majority of students into a residual category of 'other' can only have a crude level of fitness for purpose. The use of the term also indicates the paucity of our ability to classify different kinds of qualifications and learning. Attempts are being made by the LSC to make more meaningful distinctions, but much valuable provision is at risk of being lost while these processes are made operational. Confusingly, the term 'other FE' is also used by some within the sector to describe all provision that falls outside the current Government's priorities – literacy and numeracy courses leading to national tests, courses leading to a first full Level 2 qualification for adults lacking one, or to courses funded through the Employer Training Pilot (now becoming the National Employer Training Programme).

56. ***Key themes for adult learning***

    The Committee invites other stakeholders to refine or develop its new proposed typology of what it offers as the three key dimensions of adult learning in colleges: the three key roles which should be required of publicly-funded institutions of further education. Each has a different balance of claims on the public purse, on individual contribution, and on employer investment, but each we believe is essential for further education to play its full role in supporting a robust economy, individual mobility and social cohesion. The three themes, which are identified in the opening section of this Report are:

• **'Access to employability – beyond welfare'**

    This dimension of adult learning is driven primarily by government which has a proper concern to ensure that all who have completed their period of compulsory education have access to a secure skills base to play an effective part in the labour market and civil society. This is, as some of the statistical evidence in this Report indicates, a very significant part of the current work of the colleges.

● **'The learning workforce'**

Workforce development in the modern economy requires the acquisition of new skills, updating skills in existing jobs, high levels of understanding of the factors affecting business success, and career development. It is primarily the responsibility of business to secure the necessary opportunities: colleges have a key role, working with industry, in making responsive provision.

● **'Sustaining and enriching cultural value'**

Such provision is the mark of a civilised society, and is good for individuals, communities, the nation. The Blunkett preface to *The Learning Age*, quoted later in this report (para 92), sums up this dimension: "As well as securing our economic future, learning has a wider contribution." The funding of such work will change, but colleges in the present circumstances are a necessary provider of it.

57. Access to employability

Colleges will have a continuing need to support adults to gain basic skills in literacy, language and numeracy. These are a critical platform for employability, and far too many adults experience reduced options in their working lives, poorer rates of pay, greater instability in work because, in part at least, they lack such skills. John Bynner's research for the National Research and Development Centre for Literacy and Numeracy makes clear that the children of adults with skills below Entry Level 2 are most likely to replicate their parents' poor skills. People in prison have disproportionately high levels of poor literacy and especially poor numeracy, and the productivity data shows a 9 per cent lifetime enhancement in earnings for people with Level 1 numeracy skills against Entry Level 3. The economic case for investing in basic skills, and the key skills of communication, team-working and problem-solving is unanswerable, and however much success the Skills for Life Strategy continues to enjoy, there will be continuing need for such investment into the future.

58. Increased migration from East and Central Europe, and from beyond the European Union, will continue to stoke demand for provision of English for Speakers of Other Languages. So, too, will the need to engage in the labour market women from settled linguistic minority communities in the UK. Here, though, the balance of investment by the state in a basic communication skill for citizens will need to be balanced by a recognition that many economic migrants may themselves be able to pay, or persuade their employers to pay, for their language courses. At present, rising demand for ESOL courses represents a major source of funding pressure on LSC adult budgets. Total funding for ESOL rose from £170 million in 2001-2 to £256 million in 2003-4. NIACE plans to review the balance of need for ESOL provision in a separate enquiry to be launched in October 2005.

59. The focus of the Skills Strategy on people with low or no qualifications attracted widespread support when the policy was first adopted in 2003. However, much of that support was offered on the presumption that the strategy included support for all the studies progressing towards Level 2. That, certainly, will be the need for the future – to ensure that those who emerge from initial education without widely recognised qualifications (still almost 50 per cent of the cohort) should have access to the skills to secure effective labour market participation later on. It is clearly a continuing, central role of colleges to secure that access. Colleges will rely on the rapid development of a robust credit-based qualifications system to that end. Colleges will play a role, too, in offering access to employability for other groups currently marginalised from work. Those who experience substantial illness in childhood, adults with learning difficulties and/or disabilities, those recovering from mental health problems, and people on incapacity benefits seeking to return to work will all make demands on colleges.

60. In meeting the needs of adults seeking access to employability, as in other key themes highlighted in this Report, colleges will not be sole providers of publicly-funded support. However, they will need to be strategic respondents – securing partnerships with others in local

authorities, in the voluntary and community sector, and among private trainers to ensure comprehensive coverage, rigorous quality and transparent progression routes.

61. The 'learning workforce' dimension
Adults learning through employment
Government policy is clearly focused on improving the interaction between colleges and employers. Industrial and demographic change will make learning workplaces and learning organisations more necessary. But they are likely to make different demands on colleges – for customised solutions, and just-in-time training – in which the underpinning relationships will be of key importance. Initiatives like Warwickshire College's Trident Centre will become more common. The College hosts a joint venture with a cluster of industrial partners who have developed company training facilities, with advanced technology, on the college site. The Government seeks to focus strengthened employer-college links through its National Employment Training Programmes and, via a network of industry-led academies, the latest in a series of initiatives which recently saw the establishment and spread of Centres for Vocational Excellence.

62. Since vocational education is central to colleges' roles, the evidence from the enquiry survey on managers' sense of the primary purpose of their work is worrying (though, given recent history and shifts in policy, not wholly surprising). However, employer-focused developments need to complement opportunities for individuals to shape their own careers, and the evidence that between 60 and 90 per cent of Employment Training Pilot provision has funded employers for work they would otherwise have had to pay for themselves, suggests that current strategies will not secure the balance that is needed. The danger is that developing positive relations with employers will be bought directly at the expense of individuals' learning routes.

63. The newly-established Sector Skills Councils face a considerable challenge, too, in increasing direct employer investment in education and training, and in making sure that adults as well as young labour market entrants are adequately catered for. In moving towards a

future that commands wide levels of agreement, colleges (currently responsible for provision leading to more than half of all vocational qualifications awarded) should strengthen their partnerships with SSCs and with industry. They should demonstrate their capacity to build on existing good practices. But it will also be necessary for employer organisations, perhaps encouraged by government, to recognise that training is essential to their future profitability and that it needs to be paid for.

64. Government policy is very clearly that colleges must work more closely with employers through various initiatives. Ivan Lewis, until 2005 a Minister at DfES, has said that FE colleges have nothing to fear from the Employer Training Programme and that many entrepreneurial colleges were engaging with employers and providing high quality customised training (2 December 2004, oral answer to question on ETP). This is the some of the good practice that will need to be replicated.

65. **Colleges' perceptions of employer engagement**
Colleges feel that they are already responsive to employer demand (source: NIACE Consultation Survey). Some 42 per cent felt that they were good at being responsive to employers, 39 per cent felt that they were reasonable, while only 15 per cent felt that they were poor at this. Surveys conducted by the Association of Colleges show that the average GFE college has links with more than 500 employers, though it is not claimed that these numbers are reflected in those purchasing training from the college. However, a survey conducted for the LSC showed a high rate of satisfaction among employers with Centres of Vocational Excellence in colleges. Nine in ten were intending to use the college again.

66. Colleges engage with business through a range of activities, such as employer centres in college premises, joint partnership working, seconded staff for dedicated projects and distance learning schemes. However, engagement with employers is limited by other factors:
● 55 per cent felt that the chief factor that impacted upon their ability

to be responsive to local demand was funding (which again raises the question of who should pay).

- 33 per cent had difficulties with the need to provide flexible provision and the mode of delivery. A credit-based framework would help with this engagement.
- 30 per cent felt constrained by difficulties over the availability of suitable staff.
(*Source*: NIACE Consultation Survey and Case Studies)

67. These factors may influence the level of employer involvement in learner attendance on FE courses. Not surprisingly, many more adults (9 per cent) are studying with employer support than is the case for young people (2 per cent) (Source: ILR). However, it should be noted that the figure for adults backed by their employer has dropped, and in 2003-4 was only 83 per cent of the 2001-2 figure. Employer involvement may thus actually be decreasing. This ought to be a matter of concern to the colleges. Additionally, around two-thirds of all employers' training expenditure goes to commercial providers, and colleges demonstrating clear success in employer engagement are a minority. If, as this Report argues, vocational education for young people and adults is the key element in the FE mission, then some urgent development is needed among those with this aspiration.

68. It should be noted, however, that the *lower* the level of study, the more important to adults the element of vocational provision is. This has a bearing upon the 'Level 2 entitlement', as it relates to employers. As policy currently stands employers are encouraged to sign up for full Level 2 – but as the figures above illustrate, although the availability of Level 2 may become increasingly important as a progression route, the immediate need is for lower Entry and Level 1 courses, or for the ability to study towards a prospective Level 2 through easier, modularised stages. This is causing concern among providers:

"There will be a higher target for full Level 2 next year. Curriculum Centres will be coerced into targeting this market."

> "What kind of Level 2 policy is it that stops us including a bright young woman who wants one more GCSE in order to attain her L2 qualification?" – *College in the North West*

69. The Level 2 entitlement may also be harmful to the individual, through potential mismatch with the needs of the local labour market. Labour Market data (Source: *English Labour Force Survey* 2003) establishes that there are key sectors of predicted vulnerability – especially in low-skilled areas like elementary, plant and machine operation, but also in some skilled trades occupations – where the need is for Entry Level/Level 1 opportunities. Any drive to Level 2, at the expense of Entry or Level 1, would impact disproportionately upon the lowest skilled in the work force.

70. In addition to this, there is some concern among colleges that the Level 2 entitlement is having an adverse effect on some provision at Level 3, including some of that in Centres of Vocational Excellence. This is a result of the tighter funding eligibility rules that have been introduced by LSC, with consequent reductions in funding. The Learning and Skills Development Agency has conducted a research exercise among a sample of colleges with CoVE status, and has reported that many of them register concern about the new rules

> Case Studies and other submissions indicate a high degree of scepticism around the mixed messages sent out by the employer-training pilot (eg, employers should be asked to pay more yet are heavily subsidised through ETP). What should have been a change management tool has, in fact, muddied the waters, and reinforced the notion of subsidised training. Case study C (in a rural area) felt that ETP had been valuable in opening up participation in basic skills, but 97 per cent of participating organisations were SMEs so it is unlikely that they would have significant training budgets/numbers of staff, and so will not be a source of high demand in the future.

and their impact on the CoVE offer. Some are planning to offer full-cost courses, but are also expressing reservations about the willingness of employers and/or employees to pay.

71. Sustaining and enriching cultural value

Learning in the further education sector must serve the interests of employers, but that must not be allowed to become the whole story. There are many more purposes to education. Where the national aim is to lift skill levels across the workforce it is entirely reasonable that public investment should target areas of market failure, and should support the least-skilled. Equally, it is reasonable to expect that those who will benefit most from their qualifications to make a greater contribution to the costs of learning. The arguments about funding, however, must be kept separate from those about the nature of provision.

72. Learning for personal fulfilment, for growth and change, for community development, for cultural enrichment is also a good, and a necessary one. The fostering of a critical and informed awareness in the whole community is of central importance in establishing and maintaining a vibrant and engaged democracy. The Cologne Charter on the Aims and Ambitions for Lifelong Learning, 1999 is very clear about the essential contribution of vocational training and adult skills acquisition, but is equally clear that

"at all stages of learning emphasis should be given to the importance of creativity, entrepreneurship and education for democratic citizenship, including respect for the political, civil and human rights of all people, the value of tolerance and pluralism, and an understanding and respect for the diversity of different communities, views and traditions".

The Cologne Summit of the G8 Group, June 1999

73. The traditions of adult learning in Britain are very strong, and it is no part of this paper to argue that they have become less so. However, it is incontestably true that university extra-mural departments have closed, that college prospectuses have been trimmed, that oppor-

tunity is, at least for the present, reduced. In the kind of society which 21st century Britain is, increasingly diverse and multi-cultural, in which social division is apparently tending to widen rather than narrow, it is essential that the traditions are renewed and rebuilt, not further eroded. The further education colleges, key civic institutions in both urban and rural settings, are an important part of the process.

Qualifications and assessment

74. There is little argument with the proposition that there is urgent need for qualifications reform in vocational education. Employers have long been dissatisfied with what has been available, despite constant amendment and tinkering with the offer: colleges and lecturers have been constrained by successive tightly-drawn funding regimes and by inflexibility in the recognition of new qualifications from developing programmes that respond to the needs of employers and individuals. The Qualifications and Curriculum Authority is most certainly aware that the current National Qualifications Framework is neither truly national nor in any meaningful sense a framework: it is a list, now numbering over 5,000 ostensibly different qualifications, without clear guiding principle or coherence. In the words of QCA Chief Executive Ken Boston,

> "Users of the National Qualifications Framework have to navigate a sometimes confusing array of qualifications types from different awarding bodies, each with their own naming conventions…there are frequently gaps and overlaps in an occupational or subject area, making it difficult for individuals and organisations to compare qualifications, identify clear progression routes and determine which options best meet their needs."
>
> *New thinking for Reform: A Framework for Achievement*, QCA, 2004

75. It is perhaps a symptom – certainly a consequence – of the inadequacy of the current NQF that so many learners' achievements in colleges, employment, community-based and other less formal contexts are currently not recognised through existing qualifications. This situation clearly cannot be interpreted simply as failure by

learners, colleges and other providers. QCA has formally acknowledged that 'our qualifications system is not inclusive enough'.

76. The Government has given a joint remit to the QCA and the Learning and Skills Council to take forward a programme of qualifications reform. The rationale for the reform programme is that existing qualifications are too inflexible, too bureaucratic and too complex. Reform is urgently needed because

● there are too many awards, which confuse learners and employers
● there is no mechanism for including employer and private training in the framework
● qualifications are often inflexible and out of date, with long lead times for change
● learners can lose some of their achievements if they fail to complete a qualification first time round
● there is need to embrace a wider range of learning achievements.

77. Colleges have been penalised by having to operate within a system which is not fit for purpose. Like the learners identified in the fourth bullet above, they too suffer if their students fail to achieve a whole qualification, even if the student has never had the wish or the intent to take the whole qualification. Funding systems and achievement of targets and inspection gradings have all been assessed on what is essentially a false premise: that the only way to measure educational success is by counting completed qualifications. The methodology and the philosophy underlying it are too crude and not in tune with how many adults learn or would like to learn. QCA's own research reveals that "over two-thirds of learners said they would be happy to take part in learning and training if they could do it at their own pace without having to commit to a big programme".[1]

78. It can be argued that the colleges and their institutions have failed to present the case for new approaches early or strongly enough. If they have done so, their representations have not been fruitful, yet

---

1 Taken from QCA-commissioned research conducted by Opinion Leader into stakeholder views on vocational qualifications and provision, November 2004.

the colleges have been operating some qualification and assessment systems for 20 years and more which have pointed the way to more successful outcomes. It has been singularly unhelpful to English education, to vocational education and to adults in particular that the lessons have been resisted for so long.

The case for credit

79. Credit is a means of valuing and recognising all learning achievements, giving a value to coherent sets of learning achievements at a designated level. A credit-based system therefore encourages the accumulation of learning, at different times, in different places, at different speeds, all within an approved regulatory system. It encourages the individual learner who may be daunted by, or not ready for, whole programmes with examination-based assessments: it builds confidence through units of success. It enables employers with good in-house training schemes to take the option to ensure that their employees' achievements can be recognised and potentially contribute to occupational qualifications. Flexibility and responsiveness become characteristics of such a system, allowing for the inclusion of customised awards that meet specific market or employer or learner needs.

80. Consultation on the proposed new Framework for Achievement has taken place and it remains the intention that it will be 'open for business' during 2006, and fully operational by 2010. It will be credit-based, and the design features are clearly delineated on the QCA website. These key design features will be used to establish a system of credit accumulation and transfer that will underpin all qualifications in the Framework, and all qualifications in the FfA will be based on rules of combination for credit achievement. There is much yet to be done before this system will be operational – it will require very different approaches from the large number of awarding bodies which this country, almost uniquely, has seen establish themselves – but the benefits are very clear, to individuals, to companies, to training providers, to the country, as it seeks to maximise the benefits of the Skills Strategy.

The challenge to colleges

81. Colleges have long been criticised for failing to meet the needs of industry, and there can be little doubt that some of this criticism is merited. It is equally beyond doubt that they have not been helped by a qualifications system over which they have had little control and which has been highly inflexible and unresponsive. There are examples, on the other hand, where some colleges who have been highly successful in working with industry are being penalised by over-rigid funding rules which are having the effect of forcing them to reduce such work. (The question of 'who pays?' is dealt with elsewhere in this report.)

82. However, the operating environment will be changed with the Framework for Achievement. It will be possible to give employers what they want, to respond to identified demand with tailored programmes that can be constructed to form part of national qualifications if desired, or can stand alone and still receive educational credit (and funding, where appropriate.) Colleges will need to raise their game in these new circumstances, and prove themselves able to exploit the educational freedoms that follow. If they do not do so, their market share will quickly and significantly reduce, and both freedoms and funding will no longer be available, because new agencies will occupy the territory. New approaches to the potential partnerships with industry, and to curriculum innovation and design, will characterise colleges which can demonstrate their success in this field. The Committee believes that the re-definition of the mission of colleges – in relation to the economy, industry and employers – is central to their future role.

The funding of adult learning

83. Current educational spending strategies and priorities are clearly established, and college programmes for 2005-6 have been adjusted accordingly. Much provision has been redesigned in order to meet LSC directives on eligibility (the flight from 'other'). Some programmes have simply been dropped, and fees have generally been

increased in order to meet higher targets for fee income. The 2004-5-grant letter to the LSC from the then Secretary of State was very clear: the LSC would need "to work with colleges and training providers to maximise fee income". The full impact of these changes will not be seen until 2006-7, by which time the policies will have become embedded and will – on present indications – have hardened further.

84. Much provision in further education colleges has been offered at low cost to the customers in the recent past. Ruth Kelly, present Secretary of State, has referred a number of times to £100 million of uncollected fees, with the clear implication that it is up to the colleges to start bringing this money in. Approximately £48 million of this total amount is attributed to the waiving of fees for full-time adult learners: since this practice is now highly likely to stop, it can be assumed that (a) there will be fewer full-time adult learners in colleges; (b) there will be fewer courses, at least in the short term, aimed at full-time adults; and (c) the case for a loan system applicable to further education students as well as to higher education students will become much stronger.

85. The widespread practice of the waiving of fees for full-time and for many part-time adult students is, of course, the result of earlier priorities under which the colleges were funded. Much of FE has been numbers-driven: widening participation, and reaching disadvantaged and reluctant learners, have been key objectives. There have been national guidelines for fee remission, but many colleges have developed and operated their own criteria in addition. This has not been all philanthropic: the climate in which colleges were operating from 1993, after incorporation, was highly competitive, and the fear of being undercut by neighbouring colleges – especially in city areas with multiple providers – was powerful.

86. Remission is likely to be substantially less, and fees will be progressively higher. The additional immediate increase (27.5 per cent instead of 25 per cent of the cost of approved courses) is not going to cause much hardship or reduction in numbers, but in cases where

subsidy is now deemed inadmissible (as with much 'other' provision) increases are going to be much greater. Colleges will have to make the decision whether to charge the full cost of the programme or to cut it from their offer.

87. In a survey conducted for the LSC by the Learning and Skills Development Agency of a sample of colleges, most thought that there would be some decrease in enrolments at the beginning of the academic year 2005/6, and some increase in retention over the year. This is clearly based on the belief that the customer is more likely to want value for money when paying more. There remains, however, a degree of uncertainty over the likely effect of the changes, and it is difficult to isolate the issue of increased fees from other changes taking place. One complication arises out of the Level 2 entitlement policy, as a result of which the first full Level 2 qualification taken is free. Some colleges are concerned about a loss of income where they had been successfully charging for such courses.

88. There are other concerns expressed about issues relating to income from employers. If the key purpose of the further education system is seen to be economic, in the provision of vocational skills training prior to employment and of further training opportunities for those employed, the relationship with employers is critical. Colleges are frequently criticised for failing to meet the needs of employers, though they complain in turn that many employers are not good at articulating their needs. (Vocational qualifications and assessment systems are of vital importance here, and neither side of this debate is adequately served by our present arrangements.) There are nonetheless some strikingly good examples of highly successful collaborative schemes between colleges and companies, demonstrating that employers are happy to use and to pay for college services when the product is good.

89. Some difficulties are foreseen over the full implementation of the Level 2 Entitlement, and the National Employer Training Programme, both of which provide free training. Apart from the loss of income referred to above, it is argued that there are confusing and anti-

thetical messages in the offer of free training in very large national schemes at the very time that colleges are being urged to increase their fee income from employers. Reference has been made earlier to 'deadweight' in the Employer Training Pilots, where state subsidy has paid for training for which employers have previously been willing to pay.

90. There is without doubt need for a more coherent policy on fees if there is to be greater fee income in FE without adverse impact on student opportunity or institutional financial health. It is unquestioned that there is urgent need for a better balance between the state, the employment sector and individuals in contributing to the costs of education and training.

91. It would appear that some of the proposals in the LSC's Agenda for Change may offer improved practice and greater stability in this area, but the need remains for better information on fee and remission practices, clear guidance on fee income and on changing policy, and greater coherence in national fee policy. It will remain essential to allow colleges to remit fees where the cost of the course is a genuine barrier to participation. Means must also be found to ensure even-handed approaches, where local competition has tended to force course fees downwards: a regional minimum fees policy which in some way circumvents the issues around fair trading would be valuable. And Government and the employers' organisations should work together to develop a culture in which it is regarded as normal for good quality training to be conducted at the customer's expense.

The importance of lifelong learning

92. One of the questions discussed during the course of the Enquiry was whether there was need for a lifelong learning strategy as well as a skills strategy. The importance of lifelong learning was one of the main themes of the first Labour Government in 1997: *The Learning Age: a renaissance for a new Britain* was presented to Parliament in February 1998 by David Blunkett, then Secretary of State for Education (and

Employment). Everyone engaged in post-compulsory education thrilled to the rhetoric of the inspiring foreword, and it is tempting to repeat it in its entirety here, but a small section must suffice.

"As well as securing our economic future, learning has a wider contribution. It helps make ours a civilised society, develops the spiritual side of our lives and promotes active citizenship. Learning enables people to play a full part in their community. It strengthens the family, the neighbourhood and consequently the nation. It helps us fulfil our potential and opens doors to a love of music, art and literature. That is why we value learning for its own sake as well as for the equality of opportunity that it brings."

93. That was two general Elections and several Secretaries of State ago. The emphasis has changed, and although there would still no doubt be a high level of agreement with what was being said above, the emphasis in 2005 is very much more utilitarian. No-one remembers much about The Learning Age apart from the Foreword, and that but dimly. We now have the Department of Education and Skills, and much of the strategy shaping post-compulsory education and training – apart from in the field of higher education – is about skills acquisition. There are compelling reasons for this. As is well known, Britain lags behind many of its industrial competitors in the levels of skills and qualifications held by people in the workforce, and in the levels of productivity achieved. There is still a shameful deficit among the population of working age in basic life skills, adequate levels of literacy and numeracy. It is entirely right that these deficiencies should be addressed, and welcome progress is being made.

94. Now is the time for new thinking, new vocabulary. Lifelong learning is not a phased-out policy ambition; it is a reality and a necessity. In truth, it is a fact of contemporary life, but we fail to harness learning in all its forms, formal and informal, vocational and general, learning to know and learning to do. In order to maximise the enormous benefits to be gained from the realisation of the learning nation, the 'self-perpetuating learning society' of Helena Kennedy's vision (*Learning Works*, 1997), we need to stop regarding the different phases

of teaching and learning as independent and isolated, as being in some way in competition. We need to think through the organisational consequences of what learning throughout life really means.

95. Lives and careers are not linear, and educational opportunity must be structured in order to serve the complex requirements of individuals and companies operating in a knowledge-based society. The very concept of 'adult education' may no longer be helpful, because it carries too much baggage, is too simply conceptualised. Our education system is characterised by too many distinctions, most – if not all – redundant. Education systems that are relevant to modern society will not be defined by reference to a particular time of life, nor by too specific a purpose, and all learning needs to have recognised value. Personal development and skills are not wholly distinct from occupational skills: they are an essential part of them. Yet there would seem to be a real risk that personal development is being overlooked in policy. To labour the point, core skills, the so-called soft skills, are critical to both the inclusive society and to skills and economic development.

96. The promised introduction of the modularised credit-based system visualised by the QCA begins to make some of the necessary changes possible. This is a good example of the kind of radical change in our educational frameworks that is needed, but it will in itself need to be radical. The Framework for Achievement will need to be not only more flexible and responsive than the National Qualifications Framework that it will replace, but also more inclusive, more organic in the way it responds to innovative practice and learning.

97. General further education colleges are well-placed to develop the kind of structures that are required. It can be argued that they already deliver such a system, with the genuinely comprehensive nature of the mix of age and ability, of curriculum and mode, under which they operate. But they operate too much in isolation: the infrastructure is not in place. A key requirement is the credit-based qualifications system, together with a recognition that part-qualification is important and deserves to be recognised. Also within FE

there is too much variability in quality, and (especially currently) there are too many conflicting demands on college resources. Fundamentally, colleges alone cannot change the national educational culture and stimulate greater demand for learning from wider sections of society, despite all their successes in widening participation. A major policy shift is going to be required.

98. There are, perhaps, four main challenges which will need to be addressed at all levels. These are: developing incentives and motivation for adults to learn, integrating approaches to adult learning, improving the quality and variety of provision, and improving policy coherence and effectiveness. It may be that the fourth of these is the most crucial: it may also be the hardest to achieve. But it will not be possible to make real progress in the other areas without radical rethinking of policy about lifelong learning. Perhaps a target that ought to be introduced is for the numbers of adults engaged in active learning.

The wider benefits of learning

99. Reference is made at a number of points in this Report to the wider benefits to be gained from engagement in learning. There is a weight of research evidence on this issue, principally from the Centre for Research on the Wider Benefits of Learning, established at Birkbeck College London. The headline findings from the research show that involvement in learning, particularly in structured classes, makes people more likely to give up smoking, more health-aware in general, more likely to engage in exercise, and less likely to suffer from depression. It is clear that there are significant benefits in terms of the health of individuals and therefore in the costs of healthcare to the state.

100. There are measurable civic benefits, too. People engaged in learning are likely to be more racially tolerant, more interested in political processes, more likely to be involved in community activity. These studies show measurable change in the outcomes studied, and are broadly similar both by gender and by prior qualification level.

Briefly, beneficial effects on racial tolerance are indicated irrespective of the kind of course undertaken; academic and work-based courses improve life satisfaction; and those taking leisure courses are likely to show improvement in health behaviour and in civic participation. There tends to be a strong effect on political attitudes from undertaking academic courses.

101. The relevance of this work to possible changes in opportunity to engage in adult classes is obvious. Equally, any significant reduction in adult opportunity will have powerfully negative effect on the intergenerational benefits that have been demonstrated in recent years through the promotion of family learning schemes. The 'double-dealing dollar' of such schemes is far too good an investment to be put at risk.

102. Reduced participation levels in adult learning of the kinds which appear to be under threat – and there are already indications that adult participation is falling – may have consequences and indirect costs which do not appear to have been taken into account in the present planning and funding round.

103. The Committee members hope that this Report may stimulate further debate about the learning opportunities that are available to, and are necessary for, older learners; about the consequences of the possible loss of some of the infrastructure which has supported a great tradition of learning in this country; and about the wider educational needs of our diverse population. Members believe that learning for work and for life are inseparable.

Membership of the committee

Chair
Chris Hughes CBE
Former Chief Executive of Learning and Skills Development Agency

NIACE Project Co-ordinator
Colin Flint OBE
Associate Director, Further Education, NIACE

Committee Members
Wally Brown CBE, Principal, Liverpool Community College
Nadine Cartner, Head of Policy, Association of College Management
Rhiannon Evans, Director for Student and External Relations, Edge Hill College of Higher Education
Patrick Freestone, Principal, Mary Ward Centre
Leisha Fullick, Institute of Education, London University
Julian Gravatt, Director of Funding and Development, Association of Colleges
Paul Mackney, General Secretary, NATFHE
Caroline Mager, Director of Policy and Communications, LSDA
Stella Mbubaegbu, Principal, Highbury College
Ioan Morgan, Principal, Warwickshire College
David Sherlock, Chief Inspector, Adult Learning Inspectorate
Martin Tolhurst, Principal, Newham College of Further Education
Peter Vickers, Inclusive Learning Project, Joseph Priestley College of Further Education
Margaret Walsh, Curriculum Area Manager, Leicester College

Observers
Bryn Davies, Principal, Ystrad Mynach College
Mary Heslop, Foster Review Secretariat, Learning and Skills Council
Ian Nash, Further Education Editor, *Times Educational Supplement*
Nick Stuart CB, Chair of NIACE Company Board
Alan Tuckett OBE, Director, NIACE

Secretariat (from the NIACE Research and Administration teams)
Garrick Fincham
Anita Curtis
Mala Dhakk
Margaret Dunn
Raksha Mistry
Helen Plant

The Committee has taken evidence from:
Sarah Farley, Principal, Darlington College
David Sherlock, Chief Inspector, ALI
Adrian Perry OBE, Consultant and former Principal
John Brennan, Chief Executive, Association of Colleges
Karan Green, National Open College Network
Geoff Hall, Principal, New College Nottingham
Hugh David, New College Nottingham
Louise Knott, New College, Nottingham
Caroline Neville, Director of Learning, Learning and Skills Council
Susan Pember OBE, Director for Further Education, DfES
Henry Ball, LSC Director for South East Region

The Enquiry has undertaken a literature search on policy issues affecting adult learners in further education.

The Enquiry has in addition received more than 140 written submissions from colleges on issues affecting adult learners. The evidence drawn from these submissions has informed this paper.

Five colleges were invited to become the subject of case studies. Principals and senior staff were generous in the use of their time and extremely helpful in the detail they gave of their provision for adults and the changes they foresaw. Extracts from these case studies are used in the report. The colleges were:
Brooksby-Melton College
Gloucestershire College of Arts and Technology (Gloscat)
Stamford College
North Warwickshire and Hinckley College
Warwickshire College

Meetings which also informed the work of the Committee were held with:
Chris Humphries CBE (City and Guilds of London Institute)
Ken Boston AO (Qualifications and Curriculum Authority)
Nick Pearce (Institute of Public Policy Research)
Frances O'Grady and **Tom Wilson** (Trades Union Congress)

The thanks of the Committee and the Secretariat go to all the witnesses who appeared before the Committee, those who found time to be interviewed and to colleagues in all of the colleges which were visited and/or responded to the questionnaire.

Appendices

Supplementary research data

Research carried out by NIACE during the course of the enquiry yielded a considerable quantity of data about the FE sector and the past, current and future position of adults within it. The findings of this work have informed both the Committee's discussions and the final report. Summarised below are some of the key research data which have contributed to the thinking in the report, but do not appear in the main body of the text.

Appendix 1
Adult participation in FE

Between 1994-5 and 2002-3 the number of learners enrolled on Learning and Skills Council-funded further education increased by 28 per cent.

Correspondingly, the number of people with no qualification has fallen from 24.8 per cent of the adult population of working age in 1993 to 13.6 per cent in 2003. These figures strongly suggest the potential of further education to tackle existing skills needs among the adult population – potential underlined by the fact that adult learners as a group across the years 2002-3 and 2003-4 have a higher rate of achievement, when measured against their learning aims, than younger students by a margin of between 10 per cent and 12 per cent. The numbers of adult learners with no achievement or only partial achievement is also lower than that of younger students.

However, adult participation in learning is not evenly spread, in terms of either age or socio-economic class. As the table below shows, there is low participation in education among older learners. Only 3 per cent of the population aged over 55 is engaged in learning that leads towards a formal qualification. Even among the 40-54 age group (that is, individuals who may have a critical role to play in helping to fill gaps in employment), the figure is only 8.5 per cent.

Proportion of adults studying for a qualification, by age, 2003 (percentage)

	Age 20-24	Age 25-39	Age 40-54	Age 55+
Level 5	73.3	20.5	13.5	6.6
Level 4	25.2	18.8	13.2	6
Level 3	30.2	14.8	8.6	2.9
Level 2	41.4	11.3	7.8	3.1
Level 1	28.8	11.4	7.5	3.2
No Qualifications	16	5.1	2.2	0.6
All Levels	32.3	13.8	8.5	3

Source: English Local Labour Force Survey, 2003.

The NIACE surveys on adult participation in learning indicate that the class divide in learning widened between 1996 and 2004, with participation rates increasing slightly among those in the highest social categories but decreasing among all other socio-economic groups. Participation generally falls, the lower the socio-economic group, as the table below illustrates. Fifty-five per cent of people in social classes DE have had no engagement with learning since leaving full-time education, as opposed to 15 per cent in social classes AB and 36 per cent overall.

If the factors of age and social class are combined, we can see that older individuals in lower social economic groups are at greater risks of exclusion from education, and therefore from the labour market, and that this group is liable to grow as a result of demographic shifts (as the population ages).

Participation in adult learning, by socio-economic class, UK, 2004

	Total (%)	AB (%)	C1 (%)	C2 (%)	DE (%)
Current learning	19	26	26	16	11
Recent learning (in the last 3 years)	19	28	23	15	11
All current/recent learning	**38**	**54**	**49**	**32**	**23**
Past learning (more than 3 years ago)	26	32	27	29	21
None since leaving full-time education/don't know	36	15	24	39	57
Weighted base	4,902	828	1,439	1,098	1,538

Within the OECD, the UK has one of the highest rates of non-continuation in learning after compulsory education. According to the LSC, on average one in four 16-18-year-olds drops out of education and training. The UK has comparatively high attainment at higher education level but not at 'upper secondary' level (equivalent of Levels 2 and 3). The UK ranks 22 amongst OECD countries in terms of the 'proportion of the 25-35 age group with at least upper secondary qualifications (Levels 2 and 3)'.

Appendix 2
Meeting the needs of individuals

2.1 Inclusion and diversity

The social inclusion/widening participation agenda of colleges is often a critical part of the college mission to support both communities and individuals. The FE sector has hitherto been highly successful at reaching learners in parts of the community with which other providers are not as well able to engage.

For, example, the sector attracts a disproportionately high number of students from minority ethnic backgrounds (16 per cent of students against 7.9 per cent of the population in 2003-4). It is also worth noting that adult students from minority ethnic backgrounds are more likely than white British students to have no prior attainment. For them, Entry Level and Level 1 are the most important levels, raising the prospect that the current focus on Level 2 may have a negative impact on inclusion and diversity.

In terms of gender, FE attracts high levels of female participation (2.5 million females to 1.6 million males in 2003-4). From the perspective of social class, 37 per cent of adult learners in FE are eligible for widening participation uplift, with general further education colleges (GFECs) being particularly effective in this (29.3 per cent of learners in GFECs are resident in uplift postcode areas, compared to 25 per cent of the population).

FE is also good at reaching adults with disabilities, and adults who have learning difficulties.

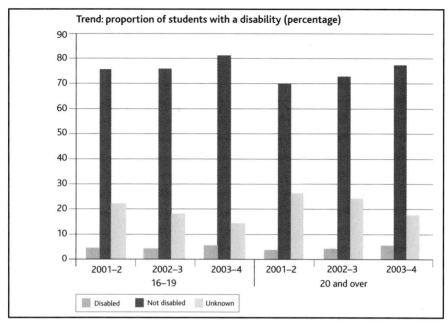

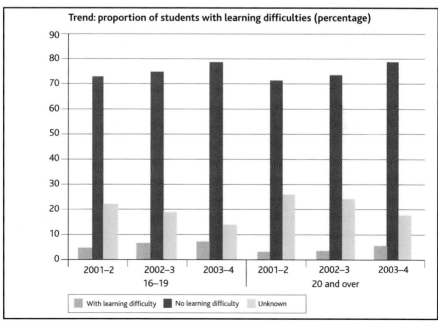

There are almost two million people aged 16-74 who are permanently sick or disabled (2001 Census), around 4.5 per cent of the 16+ population. This suggests that the number of disabled learners in FE is proportionate to the numbers of permanently sick/disabled people in the population at large.

According to the Foundation for People with Learning Difficulties, the precise number of people with learning difficulties in the UK remains unknown; estimates range from 810,000 to 2,100,000. This figure equates to between 1.4 per cent and 3.6 per cent of the UK population, suggesting that the numbers of adult learners in the FE sector with learning difficulties are proportionate to the numbers of people with learning difficulties in the population at large. Much work funded under 'FE Other' focuses specifically upon those with mental health difficulties, and research by the British Institute of Learning Difficulties suggests that the risk of mental ill-health is greater among people with learning disabilities than among the general population. This may suggest that a high proportion of FE Other funded provision aimed at those with mental health difficulties also reaches learners with learning difficulties. If this is the case, any reduction in this kind of provision will impact to a disproportionate degree upon learners with learning difficulties.

Respondents to NIACE's survey expressed concern about the likely negative impact of current planning and funding priorities on equality and diversity. For example:

'I am very concerned that our enforced reductions of adult provision will deny access to many adults from minority groups.'

'The LSC steer does try to meet diverse needs, but rigid prioritising will move funding from certain disadvantaged groups like SLDD and basic non-qualification groups."

and

'Whilst "Other provision" is being re-ascribed, there will be an impact on diversity which will, in turn, impinge on the harder-to-reach learner."

2.2 The importance of learner support

Respondents to the NIACE survey reported a range of learner support services available to adult learners, as the table below indicates:

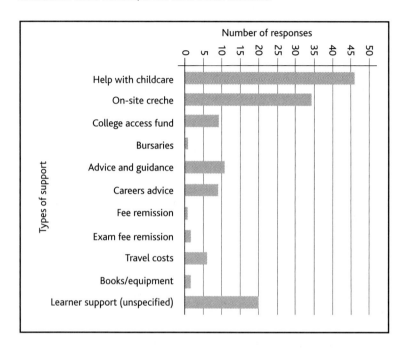

As these data show, services which provide help with childcare, whether in the form of financial assistance or on-site crèche facilities, are the most widely available form of learner support. Research repeatedly shows that the availability of accessible childcare is a critical factor in enabling adults, especially women, to engage in learning.

CASE STUDY C

Childcare has been funded from learner support fund (LFS) for 19-plus 2004-5 to a cost of £27,234. For 2005-6 £11,778 will be available. However, even in 2004-5 the sum available from LSF was insufficient and being topped-up by the hardship fund.

Appendix 3
Provision 'under threat' and the implications for adults

3.1 Adult learners and "Other" provision'
The NIACE survey found that "FE Other" represented, on average (mean), 37 per cent of provision. Of all guided learning hours (GLHs), a mean of 30 per cent were funded as "FE Other". The mean proportion of all learners on courses funded as "FE Other" was 40 per cent. The consultation exercise also asked how much of colleges'" FE Other" provision is aimed at primarily at adults, resulting in a mean of 94 per cent. A majority of respondents (27 out of 39 responses) claimed that all of their "FE Other" provision is aimed at adults. Although the category "FE Other" is contested and unstable, it appears that between 30 and 40 per cent of provision is funded as "Other". Of this, virtually all is aimed at adults. The decline of "FE Other" is thus an adult problem.

What makes up "FE Other"?
As the figure overleaf demonstrates, much "FE Other" is basic skills, disability/ mental health work, OCN-accredited, First Steps and community outreach:

Type of work funded as "FE Other"
This demonstrates that "FE Other", although often characterised as supporting leisure learning, is more often aimed at disadvantaged groups (for example, those needing basic skills or those who are disabled, or who have mental health difficulties). Evidence on progression indicates that it is often used to create a stepping-stone into more formal provision for these groups.

Case studies suggest that there may be a particular problem for the low waged (as opposed to the unemployed) learners if there are reductions in learner support funding. These learners rely heavily on access funds, which are widely perceived as being under threat, and have been used to provide a range of learner support and fee remission.

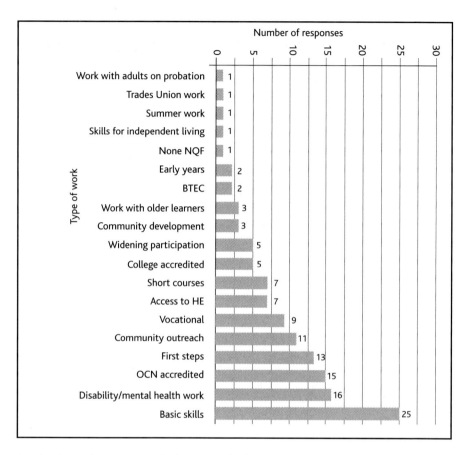

Number of responses

Type of work

Type of work	Number of responses
Work with adults on probation	1
Trades Union work	1
Summer work	1
Skills for independent living	1
None NQF	1
Early years	2
BTEC	2
Work with older learners	3
Community development	3
Widening participation	5
College accredited	5
Short courses	7
Access to HE	7
Vocational	9
Community outreach	11
First steps	13
OCN accredited	15
Disability/mental health work	16
Basic skills	25

A reduction in that provision which is currently classified as "FE Other" will not only be a principally an adult problem, but also principally a disadvantaged adult problem.

3.2 The changing balance of provision

For the vast majority of providers responding to NIACE's survey (89 per cent), the balance of provision is changing. Over a fifth explicitly stated that this would be at the expense of "Other" provision, and almost two thirds indicated that change would come, but did not indicate the consequences. This is indicative of a highly volatile period in FE provision where widespread change is occurring or will occur.

In the survey, 76 (84 per cent) of respondents indicated that at least some of their adult provision and/or support to adult learners is under threat due to current funding priorities.

The overwhelming majority of respondents (91 per cent) stated that some elements of provision aimed at adults are vulnerable in their college, and over 20 per cent of these believe that all such provision is under threat. Specific areas that have been mentioned as being under the greatest threat are:

● Crèche/childcare
● All adult work
● Learner support fund
● All 'other' work

Some colleges have sought to counter this threat by reclassifying courses as their NQF equivalent, while others have begun to charge fees.

Work undertaken by KPMG on trends in Other Provision found that colleges are anticipating an average total decline of between 20 per cent and 30 per cent. The decline is occurring over a period of two to three years, and began pro-actively a year ago. It will result in a 'sustainable' level of provision, striking a balance between colleges' ability to protect provision and LSC requirements for reduction of "Other". This figure, however, masks a high degree of variation. At one extreme a particular college has been its FE Other provision fall from 82 per cent of total provision in 2002-3 to 27 per cent by 2004-5. At the other extreme, other institutions have maintained a stable level of FE other provision, and in one case even recorded a slight increase. (Source: KPMG Field Visits)

There is a range of consequences that the pressure on FE Other is likely to produce. The KPMG work is encouraging reclassification – indeed, one college has issued specific instructions on how to recode as much as possible away from FE Other. In 16 (15 per cent) of cases, respondents explicitly stated that they have taken steps to protect vulnerable provision by reclassifying or otherwise altering the way in which it is delivered. The level of detail provided by respondents in their answers varies greatly, so it is likely that these practices are more wide-spread than this figure suggests. Eleven colleges (10 per cent) have recoded "Other Provision" so that it falls within the NQF, while five have transferred it to full-cost recovery. Respondents argued that the latter tactic is itself likely to jeopardise provision by deterring student enrolment. There is likely to be an expansion of Skills for Life and Level 2 provision at the expense of Entry Level, Level I, and non-accredited provision (source: NIACE Consultation Questionnaire, Case Studies, KPMG evidence).

FE work is projected to expand in the following areas:

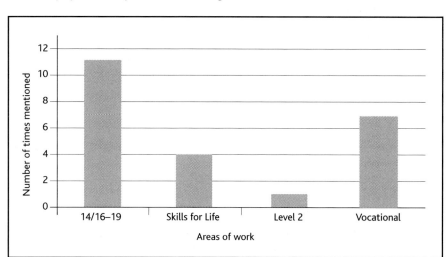

Areas of work expanding (*Source*: NIACE Consultation Questionnaire)

As the graph above shows, the current funding priorities are tending to drive colleges away from adults towards a 16-19 or vocational agenda. Many colleges believe that in the future, there will be more Level 2 and Skills for Life provision. Most feel that Entry Level/first steps/ community learning will decrease – damaging progression into the Level 2 target courses. By moving funding and support away from FE Other, which engages adults and may prepare them to progress to level two programmes, the strong possibility must exist that the Government is actually cutting the ground from under its own Level 2 target.

3.3 Community-based delivery
Community-based settings allow greater outreach into the community served by an FE institution, and represent an investment in supporting that community, and a desire to make learning available to those who are not traditional learners. The NIACE consultation survey indicates that the amount of work delivered through community-based settings was about one quarter of the whole – a substantial commitment to the second strand of what sector managers felt FE to be for (see table below). In terms of guided learning hours (GLHs), a mean of 9 per cent were delivered through community-based settings, and the mean proportion of all learners reached through work in community-based settings was 29 per cent. Evidence gathered from the questionnaires indicates that

community-based delivery represents a significant minority of work in many colleges.

Summary findings from the data are as follows:

	Work delivered through community settings as % of whole	Number of GLH delivered through community settings per institution	GLH delivered through community settings as % of whole	Number of learners reached through community settings per institution	Number of learners reached through community settings as % of whole
Mean	26%	123,788	9%	2,630	29%
Median	9%	40,464	6.5%	2,500	22%

Respondents were clear that this provision is under considerable threat as a result of current planning and funding priorities, as the chart below shows:

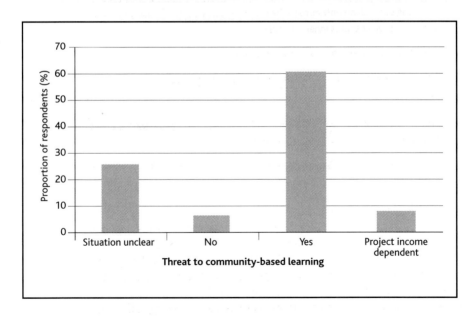

Only six per cent of respondents believed that this provision is not vulnerable. Frustration was also expressed that work that had been built up in response to previous priorities is now threatened:

> Much of our community-based work is under threat. If and when 'social inclusion' becomes fashionable again it will be almost impossible to re-establish this work.

This may impact upon the ability of colleges to reach out to the community, and specifically to under-represented/disadvantaged groups, for whom learning locally, in a friendly atmosphere, is an important way of reducing the barriers to learning. In many areas, community-based provision offers the only FE opportunity for adults in the area, and acts as 'first steps' provision for many colleges. Without this provision, it would not be possible to engage and advance a significant number of adult learners for whom conventional provision is inaccessible. In addition, to get to this position, colleges have made considerable investments in this area, in terms of both infrastructure and the building of community relationships. However, community-based provision for adults is extremely vulnerable under the current planning and funding regime. Respondents said, for example:

> '[Under threat are] First Steps non-accredited, progression accreditation – largely 'other' – e.g. confidence building, ICT, etc. Franchised partnerships, including some that contribute to the widening participation agenda, e.g. Asian Women's Project that is inner-city based.'

> 'Our main outreach centre is in a deprived ward.'

> 'Its excellence has grown provision – and this will now be lost.'

and

> 'The type of learning that we provide off site is all "other provision" and this will be phased out as level one and 2 courses are developed...'

Delivering provision through community-based settings is a particularly important way of engaging adults in learning.

3.4 Franchising

In 2004 LSC funding guidance demanded that FE colleges adopt a more rigorous approach to franchising and partnerships. In particular, the LSC wished local LSCs and providers to note that, as a steer, the maximum level of franchising, sub-contracting and partnerships should be managed so that it did not normally exceed 5 per cent of the total income of a college by 2005-6. The guidance reflected LSC concerns about 'undesirable' activities that were being perpetuated through franchising, including 'provision of poor quality and not leading towards LSC's targets or local skills priorities,' and the funding of out-of-area provision. Nevertheless, it also acknowledged that partnerships and franchising have a role to play, particularly in 'delivering for industry' and in developing specialist provision. Colleges were requested to take immediate steps to begin reducing franchise/partnership provision in line with the 5 per cent steer. The pro-active way in which colleges have approached the current situation (see decline of FE Other) suggests that a 'steer' is likely to be acted upon aggressively.

CASE STUDY C

Franchising used to make cuts. 3,000 learners in Health and Social Care in franchised provision. This has been cut, even though it was mostly Level 2 and vocational. Had to go so that money could be put in Skills for Life.

Appendix 4
Fees in FE

Different average fee levels are charged by colleges for accredited and non-accredited provision. However, both of these figures have risen above the rate of inflation in the majority of colleges.

In terms of the actual fees themselves, there is a long-term trend of rising fee levels, for both accredited and non-accredited courses. Although both types of fees show an actual decrease for last year (the last year for which figures are available), there is probably an aberration, and the large rises experienced in 2003-03 are likely to be more typical in future years. The graph below shows trends in college fee changes from 1992-93 to 2003-04 for both accredited and qualification bearing provision and non-accredited and internally accredited provision.

Changes in fees for non-accredited and internally accredited provision in all colleges, November 2002 – November 2003

Decreased	Remained the same	Increased in line with inflation	Increased above the level of inflation
1%	22%	44%	33%

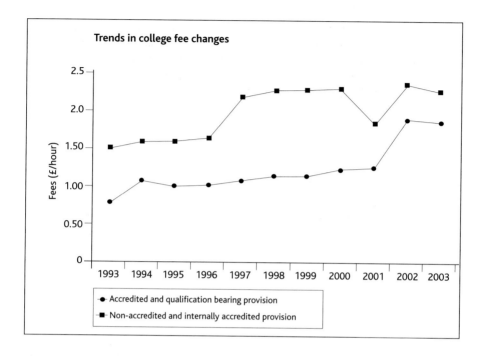

Trends in college fee changes

Accredited and qualification bearing provision
Non-accredited and internally accredited provision

Respondents providing written evidence widely expressed the view that fee increases could not be introduced because learners would not pay. One large general FE college in the North East reported that the re-introduction of fees for some areas of work had resulted in a 15 per cent reduction in participation. Instead, many colleges proposed to cut that provision which would not attract funding.

Years in college ...

0.80

2002 2003 2004